To Valerio and Alessio

Contents

Foreword

$\mathcal{I}$ met Hidi Lee when she first joined my Toastmasters group in a pursuit to improve her communication skills. I had joined Toastmasters for similar reasons many years before. My first impression was that Hidi was different. She really stood out from the crowd. Although she is diminutive in stature she is large in personality. She is not only extremely attractive, she has a completely unique sense of style that truly sets her apart. I was immediately drawn to her and shortly after our initial meeting we both found ourselves at the same 'Speakers Boot Camp'. This is when another of her unique traits came to the fore. I found out that she is refreshingly honest and direct. She speaks her mind in a most disarming way but with absolutely no malice. You can always trust Hidi to give you the unadulterated truth. She is a leader and a visionary and the kind of person that others want to be around and gravitate toward. I also find her to be ambitious, focused and driven. She is one of the most creative people I know and I love exchanging ideas with her. When I heard that Hidi intended to write a book about her vast experience in the world of lingerie, I was overjoyed and immediately offered to edit the book for her. It has been my great pleasure to do so. She is no stranger to the art of writing and expresses herself well but English is not her native language and it was my job to catch any slips. English language is a complex one in written form and this is what I could add to the book.

I know that readers will

not only enjoy the wealth of material but will also glean valuable insight into the art of seduction and learn about how lingerie plays such a big role. I have certainly learnt a lot and now look forward to more from the mind and pen of Hidi Lee.

I know that once readers have delved past the covers (pun intended) they will have more than their curiosity aroused.

Chanti Niven
Editor

Acknowledgments

I would like to thank the following groups of people who have contributed their efforts to allow this book to be published.

To those people who had contributed their real, secret life stories to this book.

To the photographer, Michael Mammano
(www.propaneproductions.com)
Front and back cover, pp.1,2,3,4,33,51,53,69,78,83,85

To the Licensed Clinical Psychologist, Jacqueline Williams, Psy.D., (www.jswilliamspsyd.com) for sharing her valuable knowledge with me during the interview.

Introduction

I remember when I was at University studying fashion design and my classmates found out that I wanted to be a lingerie designer and they laughed at me. "What are you going to design? It's just 3 triangles!" Certainly it is more than "Just 3 triangles" to me. I have always been fascinated by the thought of the items of clothing that are closest to our skins. I love the materials: the sheer lace, embroideries, the light weight jersey, mesh, chiffon, silk, the trims and even the bones and wires. I love the function and purpose and am fascinated by its history of lingerie. It has a special place in my heart. As you can tell, it is truly my passion!

Over time, lingerie has become much more than items designed purely for the purpose of basic hygienic protection. Lingerie puts a whole new spin on sexual behaviors. In this book I have included many

personal bedroom stories based on my recent research. These have been graphically described and I believe they serve as great success stories and support the case for the use of lingerie in enhancing both sexuality and sensuality. I wanted to share these, so that the reader would understand and appreciate the true value of lingerie.

To really appreciate lingerie as it is today, let's look at its history, and at the most exciting lingerie trends and designs in the marketplace.

Lingerie and the lingerie-wearer cannot be separated. Individuals may often be classified according to their choice of lingerie, based on their selection of color, fabric, style, pattern, price or even brand-name. These might be influenced by economic, political, aesthetic, social, or even religious factors. They may come consciously or unconsciously.

Lingerie offers something more than basic hygienic protection and mere physical comfort; it provides major psychological benefits as well. People express themselves through the way they dress and primarily to reveal either their individuality or conformity. Lingerie is no longer simply a material thing. It enhances the physical appearance and expresses certain unique personal qualities, thus revealing much of a person's personality, self-concept, values and attitudes.

However, there may be a marked difference between choices in outerwear and underwear, or lingerie. People dress to adapt to their environments and their clothing is influenced by political, religious or status / social reasons. They may also dress to please their own unconscious image of themselves, so as to live out their own fantasy or in some cases to hide perceived weaknesses. For example, a manager may outwardly present a powerful image with strong speech patterns and portray his status with his masculine dress style but inside, he might be of the opposite nature.

Outerwear performs a protective function and from this people derive a sense of security or confidence. It is their way to communicate what and who they are to the world around them. Their choices in clothing may also provide a bridge to their dreams or visions of what could be. Comparatively speaking, lingerie performs a rather mysterious role. It is so close to the body that it acts as a second skin and due to its intimate nature, allows the wearer to truly open up or express in new ways. They may choose what they really want; in this way ignoring any outward restrictions. For example, a transvestite might wear a masculine business suit to work in order to conform to what is socially acceptable. He may not wear what he would truly like to wear for fear that he may risk losing his job, be discriminated against or teased by others. Although he may conform to societal norms in his outer appearance, he may wear feminine lingerie beneath his masculine attire, to satisfy his true self.

It is quite true that lingerie can reveal an individual's inside world which might not easily be recognized by others who observe only what an individual chooses to present on the outside.

Lingerie may allow a woman to be true to herself on the one hand. But at the same time, allow her to subtly deceive or rather, play into a role that she wishes to fulfill. Through use of differ-

ent styles of lingerie, women may make themselves appear to be more sophisticated and refined or conversely wild, seductive and sexy. How you feel becomes who you are. The self-acceptance radiates outwardly and presents an image of who we are to the outside world. Lingerie plays a role much like a particular character's costume would in a play. It enhances performance and allows the wearer to express a certain identity. Like an actor performing on stage, lingerie of a certain style may allow an individual to get into character and perform a new role, a role that may be completely at odds with the wearer's usual identity.

It depends on one's own motivation. Certainly people do dress in order to undress. The performing attractiveness of lingerie arouses desire in the op-

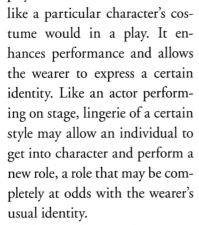

posite sex and entices them to imagine what is really hidden beneath. It encourages a strong desire to discover this mystery for one-self. This also raises admiration or even envy from members of the same sex.

Lingerie is provocative in more than one way. Its purpose and function may be contentious, but for me it truly uncovers the mystery of being human. This is what has aroused my great interest and ongoing quest for deeper knowledge about this extremely fascinating subject.

In this book, I will examine the various dynamic impacts of lingerie:

• Psychological. What is the original purpose of lingerie - protection, modesty and adornment? How one's color choice contributes to one's personality.

• The visual order of lingerie.

How lingerie is a by-product of what women represent in different societies and in different eras. How the Industrial Revolution transformed a Male-dominated Society and changed the concept of femininity and what it represents. How has body form changed due to the use of lingerie from the past until the present times?

• The changing attitudes towards lingerie under the influence of the Sexual Revolution. How lingerie is not only for our partner's pleasure, but also fulfills our own fantasies? What is the driving force behind conformity versus individuality? How lingerie has resurfaced from be-ing purely used as an "inner" garment to taking its place in the world of individual fashionable pieces.

• Global relationship problems as identified by a licensed psychologist who is a relationship expert. Guidance about how to solve common relationship problems. The universal world of lingerie. Ways to spice up your sex lives and relationships. "The Law of Attraction" in the lingerie world. The art of Seduction and the Seduction blueprint.

• Testimonials from my readers about lingerie and how it has contributed to and enhanced their personal sexual experiences.

Chapter 1   Lingerie DNA

With their superior intelligence, human beings have largely overcome in their struggle for basic survival. The satisfaction of this need has allowed us leisure time and enabled us to strive for a better life with a focus on higher needs. Before this, no clothing could be termed as lingerie (not even "underwear"). The invention of this terminology reveals that lingerie has played a particular role which has a special purpose and function, and has done so for quite some time.

There is a famous Chinese idiom that states: "When you feel full and warm enough, your thoughts will turn to sex". This so aptly demonstrates that when human's basic requirements are met, luxurious desires will come to mind. The "sex" that people desire is very much related to clothes, and more especially 'underclothes'. The Seductive Principle tells us that a partly covered body is far more attractive than a completely naked body.[1] Lingerie has thus become one of the important elements in stimulating sexual fantasy.

From a psychological point of view, the basic functions of lingerie have always been: protection, modesty & adornment.

Protection

From the earliest of times, there has been a basic physical need for protection of the body—protection from the elements, enemies, wild animals or predators and in some cases even unseen evil spirits. However, it is obvious that people's clothing does differ from one geographical location to the next. This is largely influenced by prevailing climatic conditions. Clothing is usually put on or taken off according to variations in temperature.[2] This, however, is not a hard and fast rule. Some people living in hot temperatures wear clothes while others do not.

The original function of underwear was most likely to absorb perspiration. This obviously did not satisfy man's increasing desire for "better"—to be more comfortable, good-looking, colorful, stylish, sexual or sensual. All evaluated in accordance with the moral status of their society within which they lived or social norms.

Modesty

*E*ach culture has its own way of expressing modesty; and modesty is usually governed by religious boundaries. In some of the religious, this does not necessarily mean covering up the sexual parts of the body, but will often extend to gestures, facial expressions, body posture or even social habits. In others, the whole body must be covered. Even in modern society, rules are applied in social settings. This is demonstrated in the instance where a man may be turned away at the door of a top restaurant simply for not wearing a tie. Attitudes regarding clothing come from the accumulation of experience and social orientation, not an inborn feeling or instinctual concept of body shame.[3]

In Ethiopia, some women insert discs made of wood or clay into a pierced hole in either one or both of their lips. This demonstrates her modesty and makes her desirable as a woman. If anyone tries to remove this disc from her lip, she will run off screaming with great shame.

Modesty aims passively at the prevention of disapproval, disgust, shame, disease and actively at the approval of others. It seeks to hide and divert attention, but instead of achieving this, it has succeeded in making the body appear even more attractive. It enhances sexual attraction because it both reveals and conceals the body. The mysterious and exotic images a partially covered body arouses, has led men into the powerful realm of their imaginations. It is irresistible not to think what is it underneath a Scottish kilt?

Adornment

*L*et's face it—how many people are completely happy and satisfied with their bodies? Women are especially conscious about their looks and constantly seek affirmation regarding their desirability and attractiveness to men. No matter how good-looking a woman may be, she will invariably be able to find some defect to obsess over. We all have our own set of definitions about what "beauty" actually is. Lingerie was developed to stimulate a strong desire in either the one wearing the lingerie, or in their partners, to enhance romance and match the erotic images they may already have in their minds.

Throughout the ages, the rather deceptive underclothes have greatly contributed to arouse the interest of the opposite sex. They serve to make artificial shapes seem real. So much so, that when a man is faced with a woman dressed in lingerie, he may well get the impression that her naked form is the same shape that her lingerie suggests.[4]

Some women take pride in their wonderfully sculpted bodies. They love their own shape and will enjoy gazing at themselves in the mirror. Their own image makes them feel powerful and sensual. They dress not

only to attract the opposite sex, but also to please themselves. Self-adornment demonstrates a strong love of self. However, each individual has a unique image of themselves. As we know, this is not always realistic. In fact, a woman's self-image may be a very incorrect assessment of her physical and psychological self. Women are often rather self-critical and have a rather distorted idea about how others may view them.

Nevertheless, most women enjoy living out the fantasies of their own subconscious minds. If a woman does not find herself attractive, regardless of her social status, qualifications, career achievements etc., she is likely to feel extremely insecure. This may sometimes account for the current obsession with dieting, exercising and the widespread interest in learning how to dress to camouflage perceived physical shortcomings.

Some women are affected by their menstrual periods, and even by prevailing weather or climate conditions. They may wish to dress up to look smart, sexy or attractive. Especially, after a menstrual period; a time during which most women feel bloated and unattractive. There is an urge for women to decorate themselves, to gain some level of satisfaction and to keep themselves from feeling nervous, insecure, uncomfortable, depressed and lonely. Thus, self-adornment has many positive psychological advantages.

Self adornment, such as tattoos or body piercing is seen in

various ways through different ethnic groups and cultures throughout history. In this modern day, it simply means that a woman can slip into luxurious lingerie and she feels she is all set! Whether it is for ones own personal pleasure or whether it is done in order to please her loved one, the feel-good sensation is beyond words.

Technological improvements that provide all-season environmental control by way of centrally heated homes and the increase in style-conscious affluence contribute greatly to an increased demand for lingerie. The lingerie being worn inside the home is simply for purposes of relaxation and is quite different from that worn while in the work place. Sexy lingerie worn beneath a well-tailored jacket and skirt is a kind of self-enjoyment, or secret pleasure.[5] The modern career woman may have to limit her choices in outer-dress to conform to the standards of a conservative company but might wear pink silk with lace and ribbons beneath her conservative attire. This will certainly contribute to a feeling of femininity.

Psychological facts of colors

The design industry operates around the basic elements of material, color, pattern, style, price and even brand name and advertisement of products. These elements convey unique psychological messages for the perceivers. Their combination gives rise to infinite designs and choices. What people choose very often reflects their personalities or moods at any given time.

Out of these basic elements, come the controlling factors that one uses to give an impression as these are all readily perceivable. From the psychological point of view, color depicts or represents emotion and in some cases provides strong symbolic messages. People who avoid wearing color generally avoid revealing emotion. It holds true that the choice of a certain colored garment may express a current mood or attitude, either consciously or subconsciously. The colors that appeal to an individual at given time may be very revealing of their emotional condition at the time.[6]

Generally speaking, menswear is less colorful than women's. A reason for this may be that females have traditionally assumed the more passive type—a status to be admired by others, whereas the males have traditionally assumed the role of the more active type—a viewer to appreciate others. The former tries to attract and the latter wishes to be attracted. The reverse holds true in the bird kingdom where generally the male of the species tries to attract the female and does so by displaying his bright plumage and by making outward displays designed to draw attention of a mate. Womenswear is more colorful and in fact has a much larger variation in design products than menswear for similar reasons.

As with the nature of color, some colors convey special messages and have symbolic meaning under certain special circumstances. For instance, **white** is a color that conveys an image of purity and is largely popular both for men and women in the Western world for this reason.[7] It is no surprise that this is the traditional choice of color for a wedding dress in these parts of the world where purity is a valued quality in a young bride.

Colors, however, may have different meanings in different cultures. In China, brides traditionally wear **red** and this color is also chosen for other happy ceremonies. Chinese people believe that red is a lucky color but even in the Western world, there are some who believe that wearing red lingerie on New Year's eve is good luck. In Imperial China, the color **yellow** is only to be used by the king or those considered socially superior. It is the color of "wealth" and is not to be worn by ordinary people at all. The cultural basis for color symbolism can be extremely powerful, and it is a valuable tool to have an understanding of what colors may mean in various societies.

The color **black** is probably one of the most controversial color that seems to stand apart from the others. In 1907, black lingerie, though permitted, was considered rather too exotic.[8] By the 1920's, this color was only worn by prostitutes. We may assume that perhaps its 'impure' or risqué image may have enhanced its erotic image for those who lived in what was a rather sexually inhibited society.[9] This symbolism still holds true as black lingerie continues to be considered as mysterious, and therefore sexually alluring. It increases attractiveness to the opposite sex and has become increasingly popular in modern society.

Dull, grey colors very often serve to suppress or minimize a person's appearance. That is why neutral colors such as navy blue or varying shades of grey are used for uniforms. When an individual wears a particular uniform, they indicate they belong to a group where conformity is promoted rather than individuality. Apart from having the same style, the color is also often muted. Bright colors reflect happiness, boldness and confidence. When a person feels depressed, they will usually steer away from brightly colored fabrics. The reverse also holds true. When a person feels happy, they will usually avoid subdued dark colors.

It is also fascinating how each culture has set of rules pertaining to color that may also then alter and adapt with age. My personal experience with this is rather interesting. My mother who is Chinese selects dark colors to portray her advancing maturity. As a culture, we tend to believe that dark colors are for older people. In fact, if an old lady happens to wear a brightly colored item of clothing or wears a vibrantly-patterned dress, we will find this extremely inappropriate and may even laugh behind her back. I was surprised to learn that this doesn't hold true for all cultures. My Italian ex mother-in-law, an older woman herself, used to say, "No! No! I cannot wear dark clothes anymore! You know! I am getting older now and now I need to wear bright colors! Dark colors are only for young women, like you!"

Of course individuals make their choices based on their emotions or feelings at the time that they dress. As we know, moods are subject to change for any number of reasons. It is good to bear in mind that a person's choice of clothing doesn't necessarily reflect their mood at any specific time. Whether the style that is worn conforms to, or conflicts with the current norm of society, reflects whether the individual's thinking is backward, leading, passive or active.

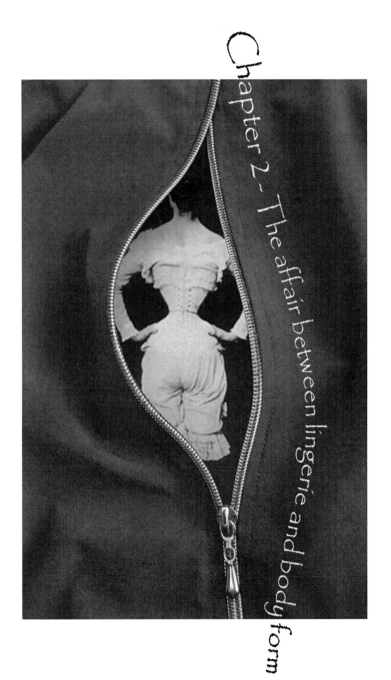

Chapter 2 - The affair between lingerie and body form

Pre-war syndrome – era of corset and crinolines

Changes in society have always had an impact upon lingerie design, reflected in its function, style and color. Those changes reflect the prevailing standards of beauty, consumption-power and economic stability of a particular period.[10]

Lingerie development is driven by the prevailing beauty-standard relating to popular body-form, which is the most important aspect of visual order for lingerie. The popularity in the body-form of lingerie evolves from "artificial" to "natural" as influenced by economic conditions, the status of women, standard-of-living, technological development and even by scientific advancement.

The corsets of the Victorian era, the practice of foot-binding in Imperial China, and even African neck rings, are extreme examples of how society and various ethnic cultures have always had their own sense of beauty and expression of social status and this aptly demonstrates that women have been prepared to go to almost any lengths to achieve a desired look. Have you ever wondered why these extreme practices have mostly been applied to women? These styles were adopted at great personal discomfort, with the ultimate aim of pleasing men. Did anyone ever consider the obvious hygienic issues? Did they think of the risks of associ-

ated health problems? In the case of corsets, internal organs were artificially sequenced, ribs were constricted and even breathing became difficult. These sorts of practices resulted in suffering to the point where many women lost even their basic survival skills, even going so far as to affect their ability to walk. Today, these women would be considered "handicapped". Imagine the extreme discomfort caused by these seemingly bizarre practices? In spite of the extreme nature of these practices of body modification, nobody seemed to care enough. In fact, the discomfort was overlooked simply because the artificial physical appearance these practices created demonstrated a woman's high social status. Women in the Victorian era for example were prone to fainting and had to carry smelling salts so that they could be revived when this happened. This just added to their feminine allure. Men liked to think of women as the weaker sex and believed that if a woman fainted she was

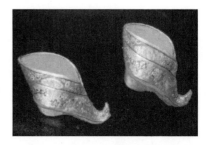

more refined and 'delicate'. This served to make him feel stronger and more masculine. Sadly, in the past, women's fashion served to make women feel manipulated, shamed or unworthy. This was most definitely a male dominated era.

In the past the physical differences between sexes greatly influenced humanity's perceptions. Men took on physically demanding jobs because of their greater size and strength. This resulted in the belief that men should be strong and develop their muscles whereas women, as the weaker sex had no need for this. Muscles on a woman were considered extremely undesirable. Many social norms therefore restricted a woman's daily activities so that she would look appropriately delicate and feminine.

Moreover, traditionally men would go out to work while "ladies" stayed at home. Most societies considered it improper for the sexes to exchange their jobs. This belief system gave men economic superiority. Women relied on men for economic support and were expected to stay at home, run the household, bear children and be subservient to their men.[11] For women going "out" was both inconvenient and socially undesirable. A woman's movements were also limited due to her restrictive style of dress. She often performed little more than an ornamental role. Women did not contribute much effort to the economy because they were not trained to do so and therefore they acquired none of the required skills.[12] The popular forms of lingerie caused not only discomfort, but ill health and even gross deformity.

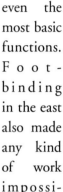

For instance, some corsets made it difficult for women to bend their bodies or to breathe properly. Some crinolines were so exaggeratedly wide that it was nearly impossible to perform even the most basic functions. Foot-binding in the east also made any kind of work impossible, except of course the obligatory work of serving their men, often done using small painful mincing steps. These social practices become so wide-spread that women lost their natural ability to survive independently. Once a young girl started the practice of lacing up into a corset, she had to keep on lacing until her waist was narrowed to the desirable tiny girth— the smaller the better. This not only narrowed the waist, it constricted the ribs and internal organs and led to weaker abdominal muscles that in turn led to back problems.[13] Women came to rely so much on men for their very survival and this allowed men to dominate. Women were seen merely as the property of men and with little practical use. They were trained to be subservient and to obey their husbands at all times. Naturally, this adopted practice gave men an advantage.[14] The Victorians favored a curvaceous hourglass figure with a full bosom, small waist and wide hips which was the ideal feminine image, representing the weaknesses of women in men's eyes.[15]

An unforgettable experience

One winter, several years ago, when I went to Paris for the "Salon International de la Lingerie" trade show, I ran into a corset fashion booth where the Parisian Corset Company had a sale of their products. There was a virtual cornucopia of wonderful fabrics and styles from which to choose. I was always a great corset enthusiast. I loved the look and construction. I was fascinated by how a woman's silhouette can be altered and enhanced in this way. Even though in almost all of my lingerie collections, there is a bustier that goes with each collection; it is quite different from a traditional corset. A bustier is far more comfortable and allows freedom of movement while the corset is very restricted and intense. No kidding! If you don't believe me, try wearing a real old-fashioned corset.

I was naturally curious to try on a corset. The French woman who served me was apparently a professional in "corsetry". She suggested that I should select one that was to my liking and try it on. I chose a black jacquard corset covered with a burgundy floral pattern and stood in front of a full sized mirror while she assisted me put it on— my first ever! I felt a great sense of exhilaration and excitement! I remember my heart pounding, as I anxiously watched and waited for my body to transform in front of my eyes. I paid close attention as she tightened my back lacing. I realized that she was demonstrating the traditional way to lace a corset. The lacing is tied up in a circle so that there are no ends. The opening is in the middle of the waistline. First she tightened the top and then moved to the bottom, a process she repeated about six times. I saw my waist narrow bit by bit each time she repeated this process. She kept on asking me if I felt ok and I replied, "Oui! Oui!" as my silhouette began to change. I could see the definition of my waist as my body took on a new curvaceous shape. I could not help but admire how the corset made me look and feel. I felt so feminine

and sexy. I guess my level of desire for this kind of self-adornment had made me numb to any physical discomfort it caused. I was so happy with how I looked that I didn't want to take off the corset. I paid her for my purchase with great delight and took a catalogue for future purchases.

It was already late and the building was about to close. I had a business dinner planned for that evening and knew I had to hurry to get back to my hotel and then get ready for the dinner. I estimated that the walk from where I was to the exit of the building would take roughly fifteen minutes. As I headed out, I began to feel a pain begin to radiate from the small of my back. I pacified myself with the thought that I looked absolutely gorgeous and would get used to the feeling. I convinced myself to just grin and bear it! I knew that I had to take the subway back to my hotel. In France, the subway is referred to as the "Metropolitan". In Paris it usually packed with people and

even in a normal situation, there have been times where I have felt claustrophobic surrounded by the milling crowds. As time went by, the pain became more intense and I began to panic. I started to wonder if I would even be able to make it back to my hotel. Fear grew, as the pain continued to intensify and I struggled to breathe. I contemplated the very real risk that I'd faint in the metro. Finally, I decided to play it safe rather than to have regrets later. I did not want to be a fashion victim. After all, I could not miss my business dinner. I stopped right in front of the sign "SORTIE", French for "EXIT", turned back to the building and looked desperately for the nearest "toilette".

When I was safely inside the ladies room, I stood in front of the mirror and desperately tried to untie the corset to relieve the now unbearable pain. I had difficulty twisting my arms around my back in order to untie the intricate lacing and the agony spread from my back area to encompass my entire body. It was possible that the pain was amplified by my great distress at the time. Tears began to pour from my eyes and finally a woman standing nearby took pity on me and offered to assist. I was more than grateful for her help. With a great deal of struggle, even for her, she was finally able to extricate my tiny body from its bondage. I remember so well the feeling of relief as my poor, bruised body was released and I finally stood exposed in front of the mirror. I felt like this French woman had literally saved my life! I thanked her profusely before I rushed to take the metro back to my hotel and on to enjoy an unencumbered dinner, awash with gratitude for my near escape.

I have never worn this corset since that time. It is now tucked away at the bottom of my lingerie drawer. Every time I see it, it reminds me of this painful experience. I know that I cannot wear it because I cannot even take it off by myself. Of course, I know that I do not need to tie my body up as tightly and I could still wear it but with looser lacing. Deep inside I know that the reason I wanted to wear a corset is to make my waistline appear tiny, and, to feel feminine and sexy. Will wearing it less tightly have the same effect? Who knows? Until I have the courage to try again, it will remain at the bottom of my drawer.

Post war effect – feminine and masculine

Along the development path of lingerie from the past to the present time, the Industrial Revolution was a critical turning point. It started in late 1700's and early 1800's in Great Britain. It transformed traditional society into the modern one through the process of industrialization. It turned the manufacturing mechanism from hand or simple machines into power-driven machinery. This helped in the development of factory organization.[16]

It sounds like it was only important in relation to economical development, but actually it also rephrased women's social status and their value to society. It took over the traditional guideline of femininity and led the world in a giant step towards a new era.

The entire economic situation improved. With this, consumption power increased and people had more time to discover things concerning themselves. Aesthetic sense was obviously changed, not only in fashion, but also in the general attitudes towards female body shape.[17] Together with the influence of doctors, who published articles highlighting the physical suffering, diseases, deformity and premature death that resulted from restrictive under-clothes.[18]

The First World War caused a revolutionary change in fashion and in attitudes toward the female body.[19] During the war, the economy was so bad that many erstwhile wealthy people went bankrupt. The loss of men led to a serious labor shortage and the slogan, "The Economy Needs Women" encouraged women to join the economic drive in order to begin the process of post-war reconstruction and intensified industrialization.[20]

Women's roles suddenly took on an important new direction. This resulted in a great step forward for equality between sexes. At the same time, the era of class distinctions broke down. Independent working women were on the increase. There was greater acceptance of the working girl and the career women.

Flat Fashion made its appearance in 1919. Its purpose was to flatten the bosom, to narrow the hips and to bypass the waist, with a boyish figure being the aim. Women wore tailor-made costumes, cut their hair and flattened their busts with their curves eliminated as much as possible. In comparison with the era of the corset and crinoline, it was a drastic change and proclaimed to the world that women were no longer to be considered the "weaker sex" in men's eyes.

CoCo Chanel was one of the foremost designers of this time and was instrumental in freeing the women from their traditional styles. She actively encouraged them to rise above their erstwhile subjectivity and subservience to men. With her independence and confident approach, she became a great role model for women at the turn of the 20th century. Her more comfortable, casual and yet still elegant clothing designs, replaced the corset fashions that were popular in previous decades.

Women in the Western world began to live their own lives with never-before enjoyed economic independence. Both outer and inner garment became less complicated, lighter in weight, and more comfortable. Designs were geared towards producing clothing that would allow mobility and provide complete freedom from restriction. The feminine body remained natural and was finally freed from all constriction or distortion. As mentioned, CoCo Chanel was one of the first designers to adapt typically masculine clothing for women's purposes. The changes in women's fashion were all about women's rights and sexual equality.

Before WWI, women had a very low social status. Womenswear was all too often constructed to manipulate women and as I mentioned before, to somehow make them feel shamed or unworthy. The corset fashion which was used as a means to measure social status, also restricted women of any movement. They were meant to be merely objects of beauty for men to enjoy. Comfort? Often this was merely an afterthought. After WWI, women were called to join the work force. With the advent of the Industrial Revolution, they started to obtain job opportunities that were previously denied them. Women stepped in and were finally acknowledged in a once male-dominated world.

In terms of clothing, due to the increasing need for freedom of movement, women were no longer bound by restrictive clothing.

The "Equality in sex"

*T*he "Women's Liberation Movement" in the 1960's and early 1970's was also a remarkable "wave" in the equalization process between the sexes. Women had suffered greatly during previous centuries. At this time, they stood up and fought for equality with men in every respect. They demanded the right to their personal independence, free from physical constraints and virtual captivity.

The movement covered a lot of causes. They fought for promotion in political, legal, economic, social, educational spheres and also for sexual equality with men. In order to gain individual rights and opportunities, they asked for more political power. They demanded the liberalization of divorce laws and for the legalization of their right for abortion, so that they had the right to decide whether or not to bear a child. They fought for equal benefits to men, such as "Equal Pay for Equal Work". They demanded reform of educational policies so that women could have the privilege of a formal education. They also asked to abolish discrimination against a women's working ability. They called for better child-care facilities and for sharing of household tasks to further free mothers and allow them to work outside the home.[21]

Largely due to this movement, women achieved a higher level of equality, both in social status and economic independence. They could finally obtain a good education that was previously only made available to men. Women proved that they could work as effectively and as competently as their male counterparts in the work place. They now had the right to follow their dreams and to determine their own future. This sense of autonomy brought a greater sense of freedom that was explicitly expressed in underwear design. The slogan "Burn the Bras" was indicative of their desire to rid themselves of all and any bondage of the body which might carry an image of perceived weakness. The expression 'The pendulum swings' comes to mind. Often styles move from one extreme to another before finding a balance somewhere in the middle. Thank goodness that these women did not succeed in their quest to eradicate the wearing of bras or I would be out of business by now!

The protest stated that "Natural" was the ideal figure shape. The current standard of beauty of that time swayed towards a completely natural, slender and physically fitted body-form. The exaggerated artificial body form was no longer desirable.[22]

Fitness and health became the focus in order to achieve the desired "Natural Look". Sports and exercises took the place of restrictive garments to shape a woman's body, improve her stature and posture and help her to gain a sense of gracefulness of movement.

Both physical exercises and lingerie aimed at smoothing and manipulating the figure, improving on nature without exaggerating natural curves or introducing any semblance of artificiality. Women's status has made dramatic changes, not only in society but also within the family unit. The "Women's Liberation Movement" that fought for the right to higher formal education certainly did pave the way towards equality of the sexes. With access to education, women were provided the opportunity to reveal their intelligence more than ever before. They had their eyes opened to the world and this allowed them to experience life in a completely new way.

"Freedom of Sexuality"

Soon after the call for equality between the sexes, came

the call for the individual's freedom to choose their own sexuality without fear of discrimination by either government or society at large. It was a call for both acceptance and tolerance. This was especially important to the homosexual.

The "Society for Sacred Sexuality" was founded on July 4th, 2004 with the purpose of bringing sexual freedom to the world. Its founding document, "The Declaration of Sexual Independence" was constructed with the purpose to free humanity of repressive values that would interfere with any growth or progress in every area of life. More especially, with regard to a person's sexuality and their personal right to choose.

Today, with input from the mass media, people have become more open-minded. There are TV shows that provide answers by sex experts to almost every kind of sexual question. The internet has provided readily accessible information for the masses about all manner of subjects, including sex and the improvement of one's sex life. Sex Education is now taught in schools and teenagers are more educated about sex and its associated risks including pregnancy and STDs. Extensive materials, including books that provide sex education, are available in book stores or can be read in the library. Couples can now research ways to enjoy one another, enhance their sensual experience and improve themselves and their relationships.

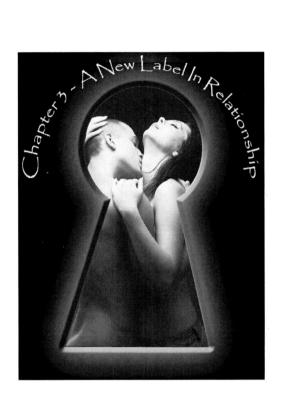

Chapter 3 - A New Label In Relationship

Lingerie virgin

People always ask, "Do you remember your first boyfriend or girlfriend?" It seems to me that this is a common question. It is the standard against which all future relationships are measured. I will replace this question with another one: "Do you remember your first piece of lingerie?"

What was your first piece of "lingerie"?

I remember I was pretty late in choosing my first bra. In fact, it was my boy friend at the time who told me that I needed to get one. I always thought that since I was very small busted, I didn't

need one. At the time, I was too embarrassed to ask him for a reason. I thought perhaps he wanted me to get a bra for reasons of modesty. Since I am a Chinese and Asians usually always have very pronounced or projected nipples, I guessed that the shape of my nipple was showing through my clothing, and this was why he wanted me to cover up.

My first trip to the lingerie shop was when I was already 19 years of age. I remember so vividly the white "Triumph" lacy triangle bra that I chose. I was very clear as to what I did not want in a bra. I did not like under-wire. Of course I didn't need that extra support and besides

I found it uncomfortable. I also did not want to have to twist my arms behind my back to hook or unhook my bra and so I chose a front closure bra. I wanted a reliable

and well-known brand because quality was, and still is, extremely important to me. I felt completely different after I put it on and looked at my transformed bust. It did enhance my petite body. I felt at that moment that I had grown up. I immediately felt more feminine and sexy. I felt that I had become a real woman – a grown woman! It's funny how a garment, even one as simple as a bra, can create a magical experience in one's own mind.

My personal interest and passion for lingerie did not have a defined time frame. I remember very well that in my early twenties I went to Marks and Spencer store and I asked myself, "Why do they hang bras upside-down here?" I did not ask anyone for an answer, and I puzzled over this for some time. The mystery remained unsolved until later when it dawned on me that these were not bras at all. They were garter belts with the now familiar triangle shape. Obviously, I was not familiar with any lingerie pieces at the time.

The problem was solved and so my education in lingerie began!

We all carry certain memories over our experience with lingerie, whether it is our first ever "virgin" experience with lingerie; or possibly even an embarrassing moment caused by lingerie; or any life-changing sexual experience for that matter. Do any of these describe your own thoughts and feelings?

The alternative underwear

*M*y gay friend told me whether a gay guy is single or not, wearing the right underwear can change his life. Underwear is a major item in the engagement of sexual experience in the gay community. The first sight of someone in his underwear can lead to the beginning of intimacy to happy endings. An interesting piece of underwear between gays is apparently a huge turn-on. It raises the blood-pressure and changes the whole atmosphere between couples. It enhances their masculinity and broadcasts male-to-male attraction.

On the other hand, the traditional white bikini briefs are considered rather boring. Remember, people who are homosexual are bolder and they are also often non-traditional. They want to have new, fun, eye-catching pieces because they are very visual by nature. Underwear has a great power of attraction, seduction, excitement and even hypnotic ability. Within the gay community, given a choice between all the different kinds of men's underwear, boxer briefs are the most popular choice, followed by briefs, bikinis, jockstraps and then thongs.

"The forbidden fruit"

*W*e all have our own unique turn-ons. Our individual sexual appetites can be vastly different. I am not naive about

BDSM. Although I myself do not practice it, at least I do know what it is. BDSM is a complex acronym. The "BD" stands for bondage and discipline. The "DS" stands for domination and submission and the "SM" stands for sadism and masochism. "BDSM" is the by-product of the mix of ingredients of "power and domination", "innocence and non-innocence" and "sexual interest". Among these, the D's are the most popular. It is for the commander to show the power and the receiver to act with total obedience. "BDSM" is the forbidden fruit,— absolutely not for everybody. However, for some people's aspects of one or both of these roles can be a huge turn-on. For other people perhaps they may be turn-offs.

I am a pretty open-minded person. I certainly am not religious in this sense; nor am I judgmental. This practice may be for those who may wish to try something a bit more spicy and exhilarating. People who practice this normally have non-traditional relationships. The rule of thumb is the combo of the Law of Attraction, conscious communication, building trust, unconditional love and acceptance, self-discipline, emotional resiliency, and more. They are possibly craving newness, excitement and experiment. It's not always so much about power and domination, as we might believe. In the lingerie world, there are many accessories that serve this market. From strappy patent leather lingerie with metal studs and rings to all kinds of other ac-

cessories such as latex, handcuffs, whips and ropes that are among the most common paraphernalia—control and power being the essential characteristics. Participants look for ways of stimulating intense feelings and sensations. Some believe that the border between pain and pleasure is bridged in this way. Participants achieve excitement not only through the behavior and activities, but also through extremely unconventional lingerie that provocatively arouses the sensory experience and allows them to role-play their fantasies.

Are you a conformist or individualist?

"*Who* am I?" "What is my purpose of life?" "Why am I here in this world?" People always seem to be searching for their identity and their place in this world.

The way we dress is one of the ways we use to define who we are. It signals to other people how they should react to us. Whether we try to stand out from the crowd, or be a part of the crowd, the way we dress speaks out on our behalf. We are constantly trying to figure out our own identity by dressing to define who we are in the eyes of others.

Each society has developed its own modesty guidance. However, modesty aims **passively** at the prevention of disapproval, disgust and shame. Any action that is against the social norm can provoke anxiety, fear and even hatred. Modesty aims **actively** towards being a part of the group and in gaining the approval of others.

Being individual means that we stand up to make a statement or to define our own cultural definitions of gender roles, femininity and sexuality. It is a sign of self-confidence and self acceptance.

All clothing expresses the concepts of either conformity or individuality. Conformity provides a sense of belonging because it fits in with the customs or the cultural habits of a society or indicates membership or association with a particular group or groups. For example, when a policeman dons his uniform this alerts others to the fact that he is part of the police force and is therefore an authority figure. Conformity creates or enhances a sense of belonging. Individuality, on the other hand, represents an expansion of oneself. It allows one to explore and escape the rigidity of conformity. It tells others that you are a unique individual and want to be treated as such. It takes courage to be different. The choice to conform or to be different may be expressed through the way we dress or in the way we behave. Before we speak a word, our clothing has already told others who we are, where we come from and for the more observant, even provided details as intimate as what we like to do in bed.

As a media for experimentation, people establish their whether the person wishes to conform or to show their individuality simply by observing the way in which they dress. Generally, a person's style expresses their personal qualities. However, please bear in mind that this is true only to a certain extent. One might follow the general agreement in outerwear

own unique identity through their dress style. They may enjoy wearing clothes in a different way to attract attention or to provide a positive impression that reflects their superior styles, taste or values. The basis of their choices might be affected by various factors including economic, explorative, political, aesthetic, social factors, customs or even religious influences.

It is easy to distinguish because of social restrictions or the value of conformity and yet, express personal choice in lingerie. This represents very real personal qualities. Lingerie has a close relationship with the wearer both from the tangible physical aspect to the psychological or more abstract aspects. It is a very private matter, which allows the wearer to be released from social boundaries and explore their own instead.

Individuality might not necessarily open to the public. It might be expressed in a person's inside world, either consciously or unconsciously. We might therefore assume that there may be people expressing conformity in their outerwear, and at the same time expressing their individuality through their lingerie as I demonstrated in the example of the transvestite at work, in my introduction.

In this fast changing world of rapid technological advancement, not only have lifestyles changed in the past two decades, beauty standards have changed as well. It's interesting that what is now viewed as "sexy" is an almost 180 degree shift from what was considered sexy in the past. I remember so well that when I was younger that profuse public hair was considered to be sexy. It created instant arousal. Nude photographic books of the past decades, featured women who were all rather bushy— the more prominent the 'patch' the sexier the woman. I do not remember exactly when this trend changed but there has been a subtle shift from the hippie look of the 60's that promoted 'au natural' to present times where the clean, groomed or even completely shaved look has become popular. Many people now consider the bushy look to be disgusting and unhygienic with the exception of a few die-hards and fetishists.

Tattoos and scars are accepted cultural behavior in certain parts of the world. It is almost required in some African cultures, whereas in other countries they may be viewed rather differently. A person may wish to express themselves in a particular way by having a tattoo on a certain part of their body. It may also demonstrate a person's desire to either conform or to be different. Tattoos often provide personal messages, while some can very personal, others may be rather generic.

When I was young tattoos were usually used to identify members of gangs. For me this was a signal to stay away. Many of the older generation may still have an association between tattoos and hardened prison inmates and for this reason find them distasteful. These days, tattoos have become a more acceptable form of self-adornment and are even considered a fashion accessory. They may be traditional graphics placed in traditional

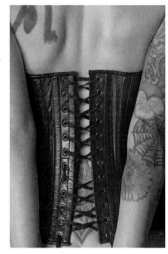

places to a very personal message in private places. Tattooing seems to have become a socially acceptable means for identifying oneself.

Underwear as outer-wear

*T*he history of underwear has come a long way. For the past 20 years, it has made dramatic changes. This is largely due to the great influence of mass media. We are all bombarded with copious images of fashion models and celebrities and encouraged to emulate their styles.

The powerful influence of celebrity is so aptly demonstrated in modern fashion. Items that were once worn under clothing are now being worn as outerwear. Madonna pioneered this movement with her unique style that emerged in the 80's. She was one of the first to wear pieces that were traditionally seen as underwear as outerwear. Jean Paul Gaultier custom designed the "cone bra" that soon became her distinguishing mark and was emulated the world over. She would be known as a trail blazer or fashion icon even though her celebrity was ostensibly gained through her music. This demonstrates the power of celebrity to influence style and start fashion trends.

Another of Madonna's unique statements was the traditional men's suit with two gaping slits on either side of the lapel, exposing the satin cups from her corset. Her garters were left dangling over the top of her tailored, conservative pin-striped, tailored trousers. A strong subliminal sexual message was provided in this way.

Her lacy black corset paired with loose fitting men's pants is another example of her unique approach to style. The garter belts were once again left dangling from her pants. Madonna was

most definitely a powerful trend-setter and changed the way women think of underwear as purely a secret pleasure.

In the past, bra straps were always concealed. At some point this changed and it became more acceptable to reveal them. Soon bra straps were made to be seen with rhinestones straps to clear gel straps with glitter inside. Women were suddenly more than willing to "show and tell".

Even men got onto the proverbial band-wagon and started to show off their underwear with the adoption a fashion trend that was initiated by rap and hip hop artists. Young men the world over began to wear sagging jeans with their boxers showing over the top. Although this trend is now fading in popularity it can still be viewed on almost every street corner.

So here we have men brazenly showing off their underwear and women doing much the same. With the popularity of the ultra low-rise jeans, girls were able to shamelessly show off their g-string. Design concentrated on details on the back of the g-string.

In the Spring 2010 Haute Couture collection, the influential fashion giant John Galliano made a massive impact by placing lingerie details before high society. Waist cinchers, garter belts, big granny's panties, corsets, retrobras— all in the

name of nostalgia! This trend is to be followed by the bold.

It is true that "underwear as outerwear" may not have translated too easily into real life. But then, the trend became more "Ready-to-wear" with designs created by top notch designers such as Dolce and Gabbana.

Even though this trend was designed for the bold, those with the right attitude who make careful selections with good taste, may use this concept and re-

transform it for use in their daily lives. This look no longer needs to be used by celebrities alone. Cleverly crafted outfits may look fresh, modern, urban, unique and trendy. When carefully translated, the underwear inspired outerwear can take on a very sophisticated look!

Individuals may be as daring or as understated as they like. The best way to translate this to reality is to take the subtle approach using layered corsets, sheer bodysuits peeking out from beneath knitwear and dresses. Select a subtle accent and combine it with more modest pieces. Look for lace, sheer fabrics, sexy cutouts, silks, slip, lingerie details, lingerie dress, bustiers, suspender belts, pants, sheer layers, bra tops, corset-inspired shirts, shorts and corsetry. A little clever layering and underwear usage can make for a great and intelligent outfit. When interpreted correctly it can spice up the entire look.

The biggest impact to "inner wear to be pulled out as outerwear" is the exposure of suspenders and stay-ups. It has inspired many bold and daring women to try out the latest sensation. Whatever your choice, these are all examples of how sensual elements from the lingerie world may successfully be translated to the outside.

Chapter 4 – The Galaxy of Lingerie & Sexuality

A touch of intimacy

 few know more than licensed psychologist Jacqueline Williams, Psy.D. about couples and relationships. Through her many years of practice, she has counseled countless couples who complain about their dysfunctional marriages.

said that the sexual activity declines dramatically after a few years of marriage.

Many couples report their passion waned during pregnancy or after childbirth. The wife or female partner begins to feel unattractive roughly around the third trimester of pregnancy. She

Most couples mention that their sexual relationship is a major contributing factor. In fact, sexual dissatisfaction is one of the main contributing factors to the current high divorce rate. It is

does not feel sexy or attractive and this may show in the way she dresses or behaves. Interest in sex may also wane. Once she has given birth, the new mother may feel overwhelmed with all the responsibilities she has in caring for her newborn. Intimacy or sex is low on the priority list. She may also be too physically exhausted to have sex and has little or no desire to conduct any form of foreplay. A lot of times, women will try to catch up their sleep when their children are sleeping. The sexual relationship declines further as the number of children increases. The woman has taken on the role of a mother, and may have less motivation to be sexy or appealing.

Another major marital issue is that couples forget that they should try to remain attractive to their partners. Men often complain that their wives "let themselves go", gain weight or stop trying to look or act sexy. This is not a uniquely female problem. Men also let go of their appearance after marriage and may gain a pot belly, stop applying after-shave or making an effort to make their wives feel good. In the early stages of a marriage, the woman may wear lingerie and act seductively but as her role changes; she may also change and no longer try to seduce her man. His attraction level drops dramatically. Lack of foreplay is also a critical issue for many couples. The daily routine of getting up, going to work, returning home, putting the kids to bed, and then going to bed, making love and falling asleep—becomes repetitive and boring.

Most cheating husbands confess that the reason why their eyes wandered was that their wives had lost interest in sex or they had given up their efforts to look or be appealing for them. At the same time, they might be easily attracted by other women who are physically attracted to them. They may be drawn to women who take good care of themselves and dress in a way that might be sexually arousing to them. This is how a marriage may go wrong. Of course these are not the only reasons but they are important ones.

Couples who are unhappy with their sexual relationship, all too often keep this buried inside and don't wish to discuss the subject. The anxiety, the disappointment and the anger just pile up and eventually they may begin to snap at one another or become hyper-critical of their partners. The marriage falls apart in front of their eyes. It often all begins with the loss of intimacy.

Dr Williams suggested that the couples should be open-minded in their relationship. Both partners are responsible to any kind of marriage issue. Couples need to nurture their relationship on a daily basis. This is especially true for long-term lovers.

We know that dissatisfaction in the sexual life is one of the main contributing factors to divorce.

As a lingerie designer, I know how important lingerie can be if used as an element to reawaken passion using the secret of allure. Lingerie is a now common in sex talk. Lingerie is a wonderful gift especially for Valentine's Day, for a birthday or for any reason that may create and inspire magical moments. It provides a subtle message, and sets off a great sexual vibration. Not to mention that it is something that both partners will enjoy. It lasts longer than a bouquet of flowers or a box of chocolate too!

Over the last twenty years, I have seen dramatic changes in the field of lingerie. Not only have materials been greatly improved, they are more com-

fortable, eco-friendly, high performance and carry different solutions for different purposes. The styling and purpose of lingerie is now extremely diversified. As designers we cater for all moods and occasions. There are lines that promote the "fun and flirty" look and lines that are fashionable, sexy, seductive and alluring. Lingerie makes women feel they can be whoever they want to be. The marked rise in the demand for "leisure" lingerie is a powerful statement that proclaims the greater demand for bedroom enhancement. Lingerie is no longer just an "undergarment", but fulfils a far more important role – to rekindle the flame and set the fire burning.

Are you a lingerie enthusiast?

*B*ut of course I am! I have been a lingerie designer for more than 20 years, and my passion for lingerie still burns hot within my veins. I know that my passion with lingerie will never die. Why? Maybe it is because I love and have a great appreciation for the human form, whether female or male. We are all beautiful creatures made by God. I enjoy the body from a visual stand-point but also psychologically. I am able to see and observe beauty beyond all social boundries. I am also insatiably curious about human behavior, and how lingerie impacts upon behavior.

Lingerie has always been a big part of my life. In my daily life I am surrounded by millions of bras, bustiers, g-strings, thongs, boy-legs, garter belts. Not to mention that I work with half-naked women all the time. I bet that any man reading this book will be envious of my job. I was basically raised in the lingerie business and am surrounded by people in the same industry. Believe me, we are a little different from people in other industries. We talk freely about lingerie and our conversation is sexual in nature and is often based on our own experiences—

the globe. Lingerie provides the hottest erotic items to enhance sex lives. It overtakes even sex toys, games, and fantasies in its ability to create and maintain arousal.

Let's take a look at what types of lingerie this industry has to offer. There are many different signature looks to each lingerie brand and each serves a unique purpose for its clients.

- "Fun and flirty" look such as "Jezebel" and "Victoria's Secret" from USA or "Myla" from UK.
- "Hint of bondage" look such as "Bordelle" from UK or "Marlie Dekkers" from Holland.
- "Feminine and luxurious" look such as "Felina" from USA, "La Perla" from Italy or "Chantal Thomass" from France.

something that may raise an eyebrow or two if anyone were to listen in. I am fully immersed in this environment, used to it and completely comfortable with it. It has become second nature to me.

I have travelled and lived in many places around the world and have come to realize that there is little difference in the impact that lingerie has in relationships between lovers across

Different price tags, different looks and absolutely different customers but they all come down to one thing – they make a woman feel feminine, full of fun, sexy and desirable. She becomes her own fantasy! It is no longer important whether she enjoys the feeling that lingerie gives her or uses it to share with her lover. If she feels confident on the inside, that confidence will radiate to the outside. She becomes a more sensual creature and therefore more desirable to the opposite sex or to the same sex for that matter.

A woman should have the complete freedom to choose whatever style that makes her feel most sexy and attractive. She should not dress purely for others but also to please herself. Nothing is sexier and more alluring than a woman who feels good about herself. She becomes what she feels. If she feels wild, then she **IS** wild. If she feels sexy, then she **IS** sexy. If she feels mysteriously attractive, then she **IS** mysteriously attractive. If she feels submissive, then she **IS** submissive. If she feels slutty, then she **IS** slutty! We become what we believe of ourselves. What can be better than this? Don't forget other lingerie accessories that include masks, collars, cuffs and even edible lingerie, sex toys, sex games, movies to stimulate sexual activities and arouse sexual desire.

I know many people who are addicted to lingerie, that spend more of their time and money on lingerie than on their entire wardrobe. What is the reason for this? Maybe these women are the only ones who truly understand the art of lingerie, seduction and sex. For most people the word 'lingerie' immediately conjures up thoughts of sex. Maybe it is the *flesh* that is exposed or the *flesh* that is hidden behind that leads them into their imaginations. Lingerie and sex to me are like twins, holding hands. Every time I give lingerie to my friends as a gift, either for Christmas, or their birthdays I am told how much they enjoyed looking at themselves in front in a mirror and they tell me that the lingerie has stimulated their sex drive and improved their sex lives. The stories go on and on.

Today, couples are far more open-minded to exploring different avenues in the bedroom. They understand the need for enjoying a satisfactory level of intimacy and eroticism. Good sexual relationships are created in so many ways. It might mean spending more time in foreplay, in private strip shows or seductive dance with sexy lingerie, use of sex toys, interactive sex games or even in watching a sexy movie together. Whatever the choice it's all about how to *"Undress me with your eyes"* and the *"Seduction blueprint"*.

Undress me with your eyes

*T*hink of your favorite celebrity. Can you imagine him undressing you with his eyes? Why not? It's all in your head, that's the power of imagination! Learn the law of "Dressing to undress".

Sometimes when I introduce myself as a lingerie designer, I have come across women who say, "Well, I am single!" as though they believe they cannot be my clients because they don't have a mate. I want to ask them, "Do you mean that you will not dress up even for yourself? How do you ever hope to attract a mate that way?" I kept on telling them, "You have to please your-self first, before you can attract and please a lover. Treat yourself nicely by dressing up to feel good about yourself. When you feel that you look good, your confidence level improves. It will radiate outwards and people will feel that from you. At the same time, you are the only one who knows what lies beneath that career suit. That silky, sensual feel between your skin and your suit speaks feminine, seductive and p o w e r f u l words to your psyche. It is powerful because you have the power of a woman, a seductress! It is an art so that when you undress in front of the mirror, your thoughts overpower

your vision. You become whatever you wish to be."

Throughout history in art, literally millions of paintings or sculptures capture the act of undressing. Indeed, it is that very moment that captivates us, takes our breaths away, makes our hearts pound and produces butterflies in our tummies.

From the Wisdom written by **Regina Brett**, 90 years old, of the *Plain Dealer*, Cleveland , Ohio "To celebrate growing older, I once wrote the 45 lessons life has taught me. It is the most requested column I've ever written." In her 21st lesson, she wrote, "Burn the candles, use the nice sheets, and wear the fancy lingerie. Don't save it for a special occasion. Today is special."

If making yourself beautiful and sexy makes you feel good about yourself, why not? After all, as the lyrics of one of Whitney Houston's songs goes, "Learn how to love yourself, it is the greatest love of all." Do enjoy the process of dressing up? If you wear wonderful sexy lingerie underneath your clothing, you will also enjoy the process of undressing. It is in the peeling off the layers that we are at our most vulnerable. But also, at our most powerful!

Undressing your lover adds another level of fun. The longer it takes the more fun it is. When you have sexy lingerie beneath your clothing, your lover will spend more time admiring your body, as he undresses you. This enhances the entire sexual experience.

For those who like to cover up a little before they take it all off. It is all about the game – the art of foreplay, of seduction and of curiosity. It works for single women as well as it works for couples. Either take your time and undress yourself slowly and seductively or have your partner undress you. This is "The Law of Leisure". It helps create a harmonious atmosphere between a couple. Enjoy!

Seduction Blueprint

*T*n social sciences, seduction is the process of deliberately enticing a person to engage. Seduction seen in a negative light, involves temptation and entice-

ment, usually sexual in nature— to lead someone astray or into a behavioral choice they would not have made if they were not in a state of sexual arousal. Seen positively, seduction is a synonym for the act of charming another, either male or female, by an appeal to their senses with the goal of reducing unfounded fears and ultimately leading to their sexual emancipation.

hints, mental teasing, cognitive treasure hunts, sparking curiosity, etc.—those things that engage the brain. Brains are turned on by puzzles. They enjoy having to figure things out.

It is for this reason that a partly covered body is far more attractive than a completely naked body. Our minds fill in the gaps and complete puzzles. Lingerie becomes one of the important elements in stimulating sexual fantasy. One of the functions of lingerie is to stimulate a subtle desire in men, in order to maintain or enhance the romance and erotic image that they hold in their minds. This is the basis of the Seduction Principle.

In the bible, sexual seduction is first mentioned in the story of Adam and Eve. Humans were able to discover from an early stage that sexual seduction is extremely powerful.

So what is the process of seduction? It is about graduated

Popular women's magazines seem to suggest that failed marriages may be due a lack of this seductive attitude. After years spent together, a completely naked body may lack the charm and mystery than a partially clad body would. Just as the thinking parts of our brain enjoy intellectual problem-solving, the visual system seems to enjoy discovering and working out hidden objects or shapes.

Whether you're trying to get someone's attention, keep their attention, motivate them to stick with something, or help them to learn more deeply and retain what they've learned, and leave something for their brain to resolve. Do something to turn their brain on. This is exactly what makes it so engaging.

In one of the issue of *Scientific American Mind*, an article

"The Neurology of Aesthetics" describe a series of "laws" of aesthetics and how they're supported by what we know of the brain. This is known as **Peekaboo** (partly revealed and partly hidden). We should not show everything. We're always trying

to leave something to the reader/learner/observer's imagination. The brain needs to figure it out, and thus enjoys the experience. Evolution has seen to it that the very act of searching for the hidden object is enjoyable. That is why toddles seem to enjoy playing "peekaboo" where an adult covers their eyes and then suddenly peeks out again. The trick

lies in the mysterious image 'behind' and it is this that arouses interest.

How many of you will admit that you are curious about what a concealed body part might look like? In some cultural practices, the original purpose of covering certain part of your body in the name of morality has actually served to achieve the reverse and instead served to arouse even greater interest. It's curiosity that is key here.

I have to confess, I am really curious about what Muslim women look like under their burkas, outfits that cover them from head to toe. Maybe it is because I once had a rather unusual experience. During one of my regular business trip to London, I went into "Harrods" – the biggest and most expensive department store in London. I was shopping in the lingerie department and had just found "Agent Provocateur" which is one of the most provocative lingerie brands in UK. There were a few Muslim women there, completely covered in black with only their eyes showing. They seemed so out of place there. I was a bit taken aback in the beginning, but soon my innate sense of curiosity was aroused. I secretly peeked at their choice of lingerie and found that they were no different to those selected by Western women. They seem to appreciate what we appreciate as well. The fact that they were completely covered made them seen even more "mysteriously desirable"!

The Law of Seduction

The Law of Seduction is the celebration of the secret power of discovery or the "peekaboo" effect. The thinking process behind the "peekaboo" is far more like a difficult puzzle and intellectual challenges. It arouses people into desiring the next level of involvement. The enhancement of curiosity to discover the parts that are hidden is downright irresistible for most.

When you are fresh into a relationship, every moment is

hot and filled with passion and excitement. But everyone knows that when the honeymoon period is over, things do change. The frequency of sexual activity goes downhill and especially when there are kids involved. To keep a relationship fresh is the responsibility of both partners. Both need to work together to bring joy, inspiration and a recharge of sexual energy that translates into the infinite enjoyment of one of life's great gifts. One of the important ingredients for many long-term lovers in achieving this is applying the principle of seduction in their relationship. I hope that this book will help with this concept.

#1 Enjoy the pillow talk!

Communication is probably the most important element in determining a successful relationship. Whether it is a "physical communication" or a "verbal communication", it vitally important in the development of a healthy relationship. Nothing can be more exciting than when a couple exchanges their fantasies. Experts often say the brain is the most powerful sexual organ in the entire body. Tell your partner how you want to be pleased or how you intend to please him / her. This will go a long way in engaging the fantasy and in creating sexual arousal.

#2 Everything adds up!

Do not think that you need a special day for romance or sexual pleasure. In fact every little thing that you do to contribute to a relationship adds up all year round. Let me share some ideas with the ladies about how they can show their man appreciation and rekindle the flame.

Start a great day by making him toast with the words "LOVE" imprinted using a toast stamp.

Surprise him by sending him a sexy message or voice-mail just to let him know how much you miss him. You don't have to get a tattoo with your partner's name on your butt. What about writing a short, racy message on his body with your eye-liner pencil? This way, when he wakes up in the morning and goes off to take his morning shower, he will see the message and hop right back in bed with you.

If he is going away for business trip, secretly put one of your unwashed thongs in his luggage, or leave him a naughty note. If he loves spaghetti, perhaps make him a dish of spaghetti with contrasting colored spaghetti displaying your special message. Tickle him sensually with your feet under the table in a restaurant. These tricks do not only apply to women. Men or women may use them effectively to titillate and arouse their significant others.

Being romantic doesn't have to be about spending money on flowers, gourmet dinners or lavish gifts. Yet it is all about the tiny little gestures you make on a daily basis that keeps the relationship fresh and strong. Even a simple touch or a little nose rub can be so romantic. In time, these simple tiny gestures will be like the little snowball that gathers snow as it rolls and becomes giant snowball. This is how you build a solid foundation in a relationship. Everyone needs to feel valued and appreciated. This is the core to a successful relationship. Use it.

#3 Get creative with sex!

To be creative, means to be out of the ordinary. Why not buy edible lingerie and invite him to eat it from your body? Too racy for you? Try it. It might surprise you how much he will enjoy this. Surprise him by setting up a *Scavenger Hunt*. Post a note at the front door with instructions that he must follow. Set yourself up as his sexy final destination. You are his reward. Maybe ask him to go to the refrigerator to get a surprise box that contains chocolate fudge body paint you have prepared ahead of time. In the fridge he might find another note telling him go to the bathroom to get the feathered tassel hidden in the drawer. Once he has collected the tassel he will be allowed to return to the bedroom only to get there to find a sign on the door that reads, "Caution! Extremely horny woman ahead! Enter at your own risk!" You, of course, will be waiting for him on the bed, wearing your sexiest lingerie or maybe if you're a little bolder, he could enter to find you playing with yourself and waiting for him to join you…At that point, let the momentum take care of the rest

#4 Staging your play!

Human have 5 senses: sight, smell, taste, touch and hearing. Each of the 5 senses consists of organs with specialized cells that have receptors for specific stimuli. These cells have links to the nervous system, and thus, to the brain. Knowing that we have all of these God-given senses, let's see how we can set the mood by employing most, if not all of these senses. To play to the sense of sight, dress your part to seduce your partner with lingerie that best flatters your body. Remember to always partly cover your body so that you leave something to the imagination whether with sexy lingerie or nothing more than a lacy eye-mask, a c-string or a pair of satin cuffs. Let him undress you,

To appeal to the sense of smell, light up scented candles or rub one another with sensual aromatic oils. Each has their own personal preference, but there are well known essential oils that are said to enhance sexual arousal. To appeal to taste, prepare some favorite finger foods that you will both enjoy and can reach from the bed. Champagne or cocktails and chocolate coated strawberries are always a winner. The sense of touch is a big part of sexual arousal. It feels good to sleep on satin sheets and have fluffy down pillows. The wonderful feel of different fabrics used in lingerie is also a great turn on, as is bare skin or the soft silkiness of hair. Romantic music will cater to the sense of hearing and serve to create a relaxing atmosphere. The scene is now set.

layer by layer, piece by piece. The things that excite a human's brain most is the part that is hidden or concealed – the part that requires work to get at. Use the concept of "peekaboo" to appeal to his imagination and draw him in.

The longer the foreplay, the more you will enjoy the sex and the more intense it will be. Your visual environment is also very important. Use the magic of dim light to create a romantic setting.

#5 Location! Location! Location!

Making love in the same spot over and over again will eventually become boring for anyone.

If at home, try different spots. Maybe on a counter top, the kitchen, the floor, the couch, the shower, even on top of the toilet, in a closet, on the dining table, in a tree house in your yard, in your jacuzzi, or even set up a camping tent at the backyard and have fun in it. So when one of you is alone at home, each part of the home will carry memories of sexual encounters that further the sexy momentum.

Outside the home, try skinny dipping at the

beach together. Tease or flirt with one another in a quiet park, or at the theater, in the back seat of your car or even try out for the "Mile High Club". The more dangerous it may appear, the more exciting it will be. If you are not daring enough to take the challenge, book a nice hotel room far from home in a romantic setting and go wild.

#6 Make yourself become his fantasy!

Don't you wonder why lingerie calendars are so hugely popular among men? Obviously, men are turned on by sexy lingerie! Indulge yourselves with some sexy lingerie and accessories. Fulfill your own fantasies first. Then, what you receive inside will exude from you and attract your lover. It might mean that you will take some sexy lingerie photos. Take them to the printer to get a calendar made and give it to partner as a Valentine's or birthday gift. Find out what he fantasizes about, his likes and the reasons why. If the reason that he likes to go to Strip Clubs is because he enjoy watching the seductiveness of a woman slowly taking off her clothes, bingo! Now you know what turns him on and you can fulfill his fantasy and strip slowly for him. If you are self-conscious, use subdued lighting and sexy lingerie that flatters your body. If he likes to watch pole dancing/ belly dancing then look for a dance club that teaches pole-dancing or belly-dancing. You can make yourself become his fantasy! When you do this, he will become yours.

Once Upon A Time

Chapter 5

#1—What it takes to forget the past

*I*t was fall, 1993 when I met Nancy. With just 2 months to go until her 24th birthday, she had only been intimate with one man, a repercussion from years of sexual abuse as a child. I was also at a vulnerable point in my life. My marriage had just ended and a few months later, my mother passed away. Nancy and I found ourselves clinging to each other like shipwreck survivors in the middle of the ocean.

The intimacy of our relationship began slowly, the first few nights we simply held each other as we slept. Making love became a matter of progressive exploration. Nancy liked to think of it as losing her *virginity*. I just knew I wanted to care for her and together, experience this new part of both of our lives.

I had big plans for her birthday. I bought her first lingerie—a satin corset, matching panties, garter and stockings. As life would have it and to our good fortune, they didn't fit! I took her with me to the store to make the exchange. For the first time, Nancy found out what it was like to have an attendant take care of her needs and helping her find the right fit and style to suit her smoldering inner sensuality.

With each new article of clothing she would open the door and pose for me watching my face for signs of excitement; she was never disappointed.

At the hotel, after she had changed and covered her secret with a tight short dress, we wrapped her in a long leather coat and took my motorcycle to a restaurant in Carlsbad, California. Nancy told me she "felt naughty" pressing up against me on the back of my bike dressed the way she was. All through dinner, she *radiated sexuality and sensuality*. She defined it as knowing that no matter what others saw on the outside, she was a *provocative sexual* animal on the inside.

Back at the hotel, I got to discover the woman she had become after years of hiding from the perceived shame of her past. This was a turning point in our lives. A major step in Nancy's life, putting the history of abuse behind her, and embracing her sexuality and passion. She will forever hold a special place in my heart.

#2 – A Special Birthday

*I*t was soon to be my husband's 30th birthday. I am a few years older than him so I remember that turning 30 was a very big deal for me. See, turning 30 started my life path in a direction which allowed me freedom and adventure in a manner in which I had never experienced before. I wanted to do something extra special for him to start his decade off in an adventurous direction too. The idea came to me because we had just started our marriage and my husband loves to give me gifts. During one of his gift ideas he gave me a beautiful pair of red patent leather shoes with leopard insoles and gold soles. It was a beautiful pair of shoes but nothing I felt daring enough to wear out in public. I loved the shoes! I placed them in my closet and I would look at them almost every morning while I would get ready for my day. Sometimes when I felt

daring I would try them on with different outfits but they would never make it past the dining room before I would walk them back to the closet.

At the end of the summer I finished a leadership program I was involved in. My girlfriend gave me a special gift as a celebration of that accomplishment. That gift ended up tying together what had began brewing in my mind from having those super hot shoes in my closet. The gift was a very lacy, naughty and kinky garment that was too hot to even bring out of the bag in public. I was very excited about it but I wasn't sure if it would even fit because it appeared to be so tiny. I contained myself and I brought the pink bag home. By the time I arrived in my room it was very clear that what I would do with these sexy pieces in my closet was to make it a memorable item for my husband.

Within a few days of that program ending and getting enough courage to go forward with this naughty *fantasy*; I contacted another girlfriend of mine who is extremely talented at bringing out the most beautiful features of a person's body, especially in the nude. One ounce of courage was all it took and I set an appointment to have a boudoir photo shoot with her. That photo shot was the most fun I had in celebrating my *femininity*. I took some of my other pieces of lingerie I had, some of which were sexy, naughty, sweet and classy. I wore my hair in my natural curls and sexy make up. Some of the pictures were super sweet and some were extremely sexy. I felt like a special princess and I could not wait to see what the finished product would be like.

What I did not expect was how I would feel physically the next day. It was actually somewhat comical when I realized I was feeling some muscles I had never felt before. The poses I used for the pictures were very sexy but they were unusual for what I would consider natural and my body was screaming at me. I do have to mention though, that the pictures were a beautiful end product and very well done by my talented friend. My husband was excitedly surprised and his 30th birthday present was a success. I had given my husband his own personal naughty book. I felt sexy!

I have since shared some of the pictures with my girlfriends. Most of the comments are as to the beauty and artistic nature of the pictures and the poses. Some of the comments are in reference to the detail and intricacies of the lingerie I am posing in. In any case, all of the comments refer to how comfortable and confident I look throughout the pictures. However the biggest impact this book has had was an inspiration for both my girlfriends and from the guys who hoped that their girlfriends or wives will one day do the same for their special birthdays.

#3–Blind Folded Maniac

$\mathcal{I}$t happened on an ordinary day. I believe that we don't need to wait for a special occasion to enjoy special sex. We went to his place after dinner. I

was well prepared, I brought my own silk black scarf with me and a whole set of specially selected lingerie that I put together from different brands. They were all black, which is my favorite color.

We spent time kissing one another and getting heated up until I knew it was the right time. I wanted to give him a wonderful surprise. I told him that I was going to *blind-fold* him with my scarf because I wanted him to concentrate on the sensory effect of feeling with his hands and to use his imagination alone. I said to him that he could not peep, but when the time came, I would ask him to go ahead and remove the scarf so that he could finally enjoy me with his eyes as well.

After I gently *blind-folded* him, I quickly undressed myself and changed into my sexy lingerie. I was dressed from head to toe. I even donned sexy *nipple tassels* that worked very well with the open-cup bra. I also wore a black retro-styled waist-cincher with lacing at the front that almost covered my entire waist since I am rather petite in size. To cover the essentials, I wore what seemed to be the world's smallest g-string, with a tiny oval shaped front. The whole set was made of silk. I felt very feminine and sexy!

When I was ready to begin, I slowly knelt in front of him. I knew that he could feel my presence and was getting excited about what was to come. Then, I held his hands to my face and let go so that he could explore at *leisure*. He instantly moved his hands from my face and slowly down until he reached my breasts. His face registered surprise when he made contact with my *nipple tassels*. At that moment, I could feel the fire inside of him build and his lips partially opened. I knew that he was enjoying the feel of me with his hands coupled with his very vivid imagination. Slowly he moved his hands around to my

open-cup bra and his passion became even more intense. I knew that it was going to be a very sexy evening.

His hands slowly moved down to my waist and his forehead creased in a frown, registering his surprise. I guess he had never felt a waist-cincher before. That moment was a little "still", but his curiosity got the better of him. Finally, he reached his destination as his fingers moved to my crotch to touch the tiny piece of fabric there. He could obviously feel my own warmth and the wetness. I was just as excited by his slow exploration and the feeling of power it gave me knowing I could turn him on so much. His hands moved around the back to cradle and caress my butt cheeks. He reveled in the feeling of the exposed soft skin.

At that point I stopped his wandering hands and told him that I would leave for a little while. I told him that he needed to remain completely still until

I gave the word and he could remove the scarf covering his eyes. I wanted him to be filled with anticipation to the point of fever.

I climbed up onto the coffee table that was in front of him, set up my sexy post and then *seductively* whispered to him, "Now, you can remove the scarf". He quickly removed it to find me dancing *seductively* on top of his coffee table with my *nipple tassels* playfully swinging from side to side. He immediately jumped up to wrap his arms around me and to press his body tight against me, obviously now impatient to have his way with me. Although his arousal was at fever pitch at this point, he took his time examining every single piece of lingerie that I had on my body and savored slowly and he undressed me, piece by piece... That was just the beginning of our unforgettably sexy, hot evening...

#4—The mysterious underwear from the laundry room

*A*t first I thought it was a swimsuit. Outside of an International Male catalogue, I had never seen underwear made from swimsuit fabric in real life. The label on the inside of the elastic said it was underwear, but the brand name was stitched just below the inside and some of the letters were missing. All that was left was an "h," "m," and "e." The paid looked somewhat funny because it had a small white cross on the left just above the leg elastic. The manufacturer included an extra patch of fabric ringed by elastic in front that defeated the regular underwear's purpose of holding everything in place— immobile. Instead of holding everything tight, and compressed against my body; I felt unslung.

Illuminated by my dimmed desk lamp, I stretched the leg elastic between my fingers, and ran my fingers to from the left side to the center. Not that it needed it because the material was so tight and sheer. From the tightness of the leg elastic, I guessed the waist elastic was worn out because it was so much looser than the leg elastic and the extra elastic piece that most u n d e r w e a r did not have that went around my balls and over my shaft. I found my m y s t e r y u n d e r w e a r in my dorm's

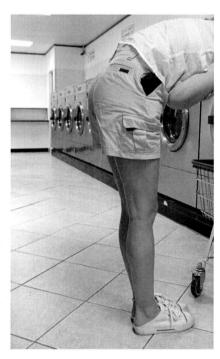

laundry room. It was in my load by accident when I carried my load from the washing machine. I quickly shoved the underwear in between a pile of Fruit of the Looms before anyone noticed. I hope nobody noticed.

Once I got back to my dorm room, I pulled out a copy of the *International Male Catalogue* from deep beneath my mattress to locate the particular underwear that came into my posses-sion. This was before the promulgation of the web and person-al computers were still not as common as cheap stereo systems; so to get the *Inter-national Male Catalogue* I had to break away from a group to a small store on a side street less travelled by typical Texan boys in New York's Village. I flipped through page after page of men with large pecs, arms, and legs; small waists, and scraps of fab-ric that would get you arrested if your "wore" it on a Galveston Beach. My body looked far from one of those models. I felt ill equipped to be gay, if I had to look like one of the bulked up International Male models. I felt thin, unsexy, and average.

My roommate had gone home for the weekend so I decided to try on the skimpy underwear, as there was little chance of someone walking in on me. I wanted to see if wearing underwear like this made me feel like one of those guys in the catalogue. Would my body feel larger? Would I suddenly gain a secret confidence if I was the only guy in a sea of Jockeys wearing "h", "m", "e" underwear with missing letters. My leg felt like a tree going into the underwear. Despite the large label, there seemed to be less than half the fabric of a regular pair of underwear. It was hard to believe that both legs had to go into the underwear. Missing was the part between the top of my pubes and just below the belly button. Scraps of fabric that should have covered my butt also seemed to be missing,

as well as additional fabric that should have been below the sides that hung on my hips.

I panicked for a second that my roommate would unexpectedly walk in having forgotten a textbook, or that he gave his keys to everyone in the entire dorm and asked them to walk-in exactly at 10:15 PM so that everyone would see his closeted gay roommate staring at himself in a mirror, wearing a found pair of *unhygienic* underwear. I turned away from the mirror and slumped into bed as the fear broke. Then, closed my eyes. I suddenly found myself focusing less on how I looked and more on how I felt.

I felt sexy for the first time ever. I expected to transform into an old Latino guy in the beach wearing too tight speedos, but the opposite happened. With my eyes closed, my imagination traced the obscured contours of my body "covered" by the found underwear, and the phantom touch felt good. From there, my imaginary fingers circled down my legs, hesitatingly up my sides, and then finally across my stomach and chest. I never turned my imagination on like that. It felt good, and I felt *desirable*. I would have never have thought to do this in my bulk-bought Target Fruit of the Looms. Although I would never look like one, I discovered secrets probably closely guarded by International Male Models: you did not have to look like one to be desirable. All you had to do was wear their underwear.

#5–The marriage saver

Several years ago my wife and I were having marital problems that, in part, were due to our lack of romance. I used to be the kind of individual that considered lingerie something that pin up girls wore in calendars and that guys hung up in their tool sheds for decoration. I never considered it anything other than a fantasy associated with men's and women's maga-

zines, separate from the reality of our everyday normal lives. I was to learn, partly due to therapy and partly due to a gift, that lingerie would become the instrument to our marital renaissance. Most people think that going to a psychiatric therapist means you are going crazy. Well, it may be partly true, but it is also true that a lot of our problems are due to a lack of understanding in our own minds. Not being a well-centered human being, learning techniques to help re-wire my brain was the first step.

A very dear friend's gift was the second important step. One evening after work while I sat watching television, my wife came out of her closet looking like a pin up girl! Well, I guess timing is everything, because between the re-wiring of my brain and the beautiful fantasy before me (my wife no less!) I immediately felt the sexual stimulation that was missing before. My wife and I both indulged in the mutual satisfaction of a well orchestrated *sexual* encounter, acting our parts in the fantasy created by the gift. If I ever have the opportunity to help someone with marriage problems, there will be two parts to my wisdom. First, get a good therapist to re-wire your brain, and second, give them a gift of lingerie.

#6–The manifestation of a gay guy

As you may already know, Sex is found on a man's mind quite regularly. Romance in a relationship is usually a requirement when women are involved (yes, I'm obviously generalizing a little)... But being gay, I've noticed how fornicating is as easy as getting a loaf of bread at the corner store on a Sunday morning.

All you need is a little drive to get off Facebook and a nice pair of underwear and you're in business. Underwear!? You say? Know this... I have spent more time shopping for briefs, boxers,

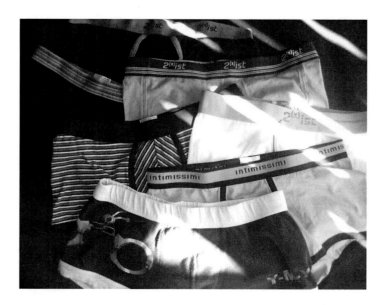

boxer briefs, men bikinis and thongs then any other article of clothing in my closet. "Why?" you ask.

Two reasons: First, gay clubs are by far the most popular pick-up scenes on planet Earth! And if you've ever found yourself in one of those strange, loud, hot and sweaty places, you'd know how quickly men some-how, somewhere lose their entire wardrobe ending up in nothing else but a really cute little piece of underwear. Of course having a six pack will help, but the un-derwear is absolutely always the cherry on the cake for any men seeking visual entertainment. It is when the mind goes wild with possibilities, as you never know what in the world you'll uncover!

The second reason I dedi-cate most of my shopping ex-perience to the hidden piece, is because much fun has to do with that very thin layer of fabric be-tween my skin and my partner's mouth. The beauty and qual-ity of the underwear determines how much time is dedicated to *foreplay*. The cuter the underwear, the longer they stay on, the more fun we get to have. It's surprising how quickly things can come to an unfortunate end when one of us discovers a pair of plain and boring tighty-whiteys!

As my good friend Hidi always says, it is not what you can see with your eyes, but rather only that which you can imagine with your mind that turns your nipples hard... Well, that's not exactly what she says, but you get the point.

Simply remember this, the only way you can get to a men's heaven is through their underwear. And if he's not wearing any, it's just not as fun! So next time you slip something on, spend a quick moment to think of who just may be ripping them off.

#7–For my eyes ONLY!

I do think Lingerie / Dessous deserve a special place in our time, because of our non-stop self exposure via Facebook, Twitter, Myspace, Youtube, and Vimeo.

For me to wear spiffy and high quality Lingerie feels like a refuge or sanctuary. A statement against my fast moving surrounding filled with idle chatter, gossip and noise pollution.

I feel good, relaxed and save, because I am protected from the inside out. Nobody knows what I am wearing "down under", it's my little secret. I don't want to be exposed all the time. Privacy seems not to have priority these days. In case you didn't know, I'm a renaissance man.

I might only wear boxer shorts aka loose boxers, but beautiful ones. It feels good, re-assuring, it makes me feel confident. I can breathe and my life slows down. Most of my life I wore loose boxer shorts. Why do men wear boxer briefs, tight boxers, trunks or even briefs? I do not know.

There is no better solution for male underwear than loose boxers, except wearing nothing of course. I am in love with my

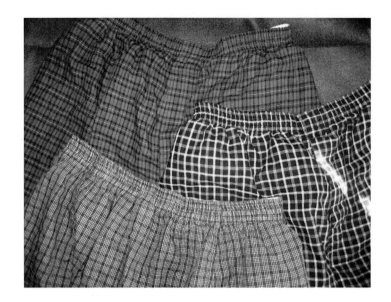

boxers and I can't imagine wearing anything else on my skin.

I do find wearing boxers very sexy, especially by the female gender. Don't get me wrong, I do like panties & bra's of course too. Sexy lingerie is as important as a great *foreplay*. Without any spiffy lingerie there is no sex life for me. It's a crucial part of my sexual relationship.

Sex is healthy for your body and mind. It's free…most of the time, and fun. So fellows, go out there and get your wife, lover, or even mistress some sexy and fabulous lingerie, will you?

#8–Hot tub adventure

*T*he line between reality and *fantasy* is often blurred when it comes to *sexuality* and lingerie for me when I was young, lingerie was all about me. I bought what I wanted to see my girl in. Then one day I listened to her when she was buying lingerie for herself. She said to the lady, "I don't like the spaghetti straps, and prefer French cut sleeves, I love the cami-tops just not the straps..." that day changed my life. From that point forward I knew what she wanted and found the more I bought her of the style she liked, the more she would wear it. Our sex life, improved dramatically as well. See the thin straps of a regular cami-top made her self-conscious of her arms (she thought her arms were fat evidently) with the French cut sleeves she felt SEXY... and the sexier she felt the more interested in sex she became. The result, I listened more and more to what my girlfriends wanted in terms of Lingerie. Now and I am happy to report each of us was happier as a result.

Fast forward to my life as a 40s adult. I was blessed by the act of a wonderful woman in a happy surprise. I was on my first date. We were discussing Halloween costumes which somehow quickly lead to lingerie, I vaguely remember saying I like the type of lingerie that has the garter straps, and that thigh high stockings were very sexy. I

mentioned that I had fantasized about that outfit my entire life. The amazing part of this conversation comes two days later. She comes to meet me and after dinner and a hot tub, steps into the other room to change. She comes out to unveil that she is wearing a very sexy black and pink corset matching panties and garter straps connecting to the very sexy thigh high stockings. Needless to say, I was amazed; very turned on, and the sex that night was amazing!!! The conversation we had about this was very brief. I had no idea she was listening that closely, but she was listening and took action. That day my Fantasy became a Reality. I am forever grateful for the memory and blessed for the wonderful gifts she gave me that night.

#9–Exposure but not in a dark room

*I*n my late teens I won a modeling contest 'Madamoiselle Vogue' and among my prizes was a modeling contract from one of the most reputable modeling houses in the world. Many girls would jump at this opportunity but I had my mind set on other pursuits and had no interest in modeling. Ironically some years later, in my 20's a need for extra cash drove me to take on a few photographic mod-

eling shoots. I modeled mainly jewelry showing my face and some of the décolletage area. The pay was fairly modest but soon the offers came in, including one that offered substantially more than I was used to. I had no idea at the time that it was going to be a sexy shoot albeit with no nudity. I almost headed for the door when I first saw examples of the photographer's work. This was little more than pornography to my mind. How could I pose in barely-there outfits and show all that flesh? This was not my first exposure to lingerie. I did have a collection of sexy French lace underwear and enjoyed wearing it all but to expose myself to the camera in this way seemed almost unthinkable for me. Fortunately, the photographer was able to put me at ease, and since I really needed the money, I decided to go ahead with the shoot.

In the beginning I was very stiff and posed much like a mannequin model that you'd find in a shop-front window. After a time I loosened up and the lingerie seemed to take on a life of its own. I found that the sexy fabrics and designs made me feel sexy and soon I began to manifest my own sexy inner beast. There were photographs taken that depicted a more innocent allure. One that I remember in particular was captured at a window with light shining through and illuminating my silhouette beneath an almost transparent fabric. My firm, young breasts were perfectly outlined in the light. It was beautiful

and suspenders that made me feel extremely wicked. The photo captured a wicked smile, eyes heavy lidded with passion. I couldn't believe it was me. Could I be so sensual and sexy? I certainly felt it.

The end results of the shoot were spectacular. Even more wonderful was what I learned about myself that day, and how this translated through my behavior from then on. I began to collect interesting pieces that reflected

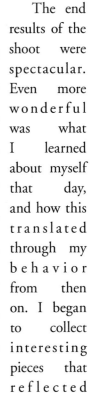

and yet extremely sensual at the same time. Others were more erotic in nature. I remember the red corset with black trim my individual taste and would wear them under my work clothes. I learned that the art of *seduction* involves a promise of something more. It is not the flagrant flaunting of your female assets but a subtle hint of what might be there. I have found that although men stare at women who wear clothing that leaves very little the imagination, they are more drawn to women who know how to display their sexuality in more subtle ways. A hint of *cleavage* and the shape of a nipple behind a silky blouse is far more alluring than a too-tight tiny top with breasts spilling out. A form-fitting skirt with perhaps a slit that reveals just a flash of leg when a woman walks is far more interesting than a mini skirt that barely covers the crotch area. Even more intriguing to men is a hint of shape without full exposure which is why sheer fabrics are so effective. Men love mystery; and the more mysterious you appear, the more alluring.

Needless to say the lingerie shoot was just the beginning of my *sexual liberation* and I can tell you that my husband was quite happy to be artfully *seduced* and remained under my spell. As we get older and gravity takes hold transforming a once youthful, firm body into a more mature one, we need to learn how to use lingerie to conceal our flaws while emphasizing our assets. We also learn that what is between our ears is far sexier than what is between our legs.

Postscript

$\mathcal{I}$ have designed lingerie for more than 20 years, and my passion for lingerie has not waned one bit. If anything it still burns as hot within me as it ever did. Instead of losing interest, I have only grown to greater levels of passion. For me, the fascination is two-fold. I love the way lingerie looks and makes people feel. I have also seen on a deeper level how lingerie relates to, and impacts upon human behavior. To me the human mind is a treasure trove of secrets to be unlocked and explored. Lingerie is not simply a visual form. It has mysterious powers that greatly affect both the wearer and the observer. This is why I decided to write and publish this book. I wanted to share my mysterious world with my readers and remind people how important lingerie is in our daily lives, and how important it is to society as a whole.

When most people think of lingerie, they tend to relate it to sex and nudity but I want people to come to know that lingerie has a different dimension that few are aware of. Lingerie was developed from a very solid cultural background and has been constantly changing and evolving along with changes in society. This includes the great advances in technology that has provided us greater exposure than ever to mass media. In turn, mass media has altered our perceptions and irrevocably altered the way we relate to "fashion and lingerie". The different elements of lingerie that include reasons of modesty, religious purposes and function are constantly revising their blueprints.

I would strongly encourage you to read my blog at **www.lingerissimi.com**. It is an intellectual dimension within the sensual world of lingerie. I started it mid August 2010 and it has been very successful. I have received such great feedback about my articles – my selection of words, my thoughts, my rich resources, and the artistic sense of these articles. Enjoy and please offer your own thoughts.

If you have any personal stories about your experiences with lingerie that you would like to share with me, please email me at: hidi@lingerissimi.com

Thank you very much for your support!

Sincerely yours,

Hidi

References

1. Mary Kefger and Phyllis Touchie, *Individuality*, (4th ed. 1986), pp64-68

2. Mary Kefger and Phyllis Touchie, *Individuality*, (4th ed. 1986), pp56-62

3. Morgan King, *Introduction to psychology*, pp89-92

4. Cecil Saint-Laurant, *A History of Women's Underwear*, (Times Editions), pp54

5. Sarah Mower, *"Lingerie Now, Adventure in the underworld"*, British Vogue, June 1988, pp186

6. Mary Kefger and Phyllis Touchie, *Individuality*, (4th ed. 1986), pp26

7. E.T Renbourn, *Materials and Clothing in Health and Disease*, (London, H.K. Lewis, 1972), pp23

8. Ernstine Carter, *The Changing World of Fashion*, (London: Weidenfeld and Nicolson, 1977), pp215

9. Cecil Saint-Laurant, *A History of Women's Underwear*, (Times Editions), pp173

10. "Small Talk on Women's Underwear", fashion Magazine, 1987, pp15

11. The World Book Encyclopedia 21, (Field Enterprises Educational Corporation, 1973) pp216

12. Valeria Steele, *Fashion and Eroticism*, pp94

13. Elizabeth Swing, Fashion in Underwear, (London, Batsford, 1971) pp52

14. The World Book Encyclopedia 21, (Field Enterprises Educational Corporation, 1973) pp217

15. Valeria Steele, *Fashion and Eroticism*, pp218

16. The World Book Encyclopedia, (Field Enterprises Educational Corporation, 1973) pp186

17. Valeria Steele, *Fashion and Eroticism*, pp225

18. Elizabeth Swing, *Fashion in Underwear*, pp52

19. Valeria Steele, *Fashion and Eroticism*, pp225

20. Marxism Communism and Western Society, (Herder and Herder, 1972), pp346

21. The World Book Encyclopedia 21, (Field Enterprises Educational Corporation, 1973), pp320

22. Mary Kefger, *Individuality*, pp195

Index

enhance, enhancement, 11, 15, 22, 34, 35, 37, 50, 51, 55, 56, 63
enthusiast, 22, 50
equalization, equal, equality, 28
erotic, eroticism, 11, 15, 51, 53, 56, 85
ethnic, 19

F
fantasy, fantasies, 2, 9, 12, 51, 56, 60, 64, 65
fascinating, fascination, 4, 15, 22, 87
feminine, femininity , 3, 5, 13, 20, 22, 23, 25, 34, 37, 51, 52, 54
fetishists, 39
flagrant, 86
flaunting, 86
flirty, flirt, 50, 51, 64
foot-binding, 19, 21
foreplay, 48, 53, 55, 63
fornicating , 79

G
garter belts, 41, 42

H

hip hop, 41
homosexual, 35
hourglass, 22
hygienic, unhygienic, 1, 2, 19, 77

I
illuminating, 85
imagination, 52, 74, 86
individuality, individual, individualist, 2, 3, 5, 12, 14, 15, 16, 28, 30, 35, 37, 38, 39
indulged, 79
Industrial Revolution, 5, 25
intimacy, 47

K
kinky, 71

L
leisure, 9, 74
liberation, 28, 29, 86

M
male-dominated, 5, 28
manipulated, 20, 29
mannequin, 84
masculine, masculinity, 2, 25, 35
modesty, 4, 9, 10, 33, 37

morality, 58

mystery, mysterious, mysteriously, 3, 4, 10, 15, 52, 57, 59, 87

N

naked, 9

naughty, 70, 71

nipples , 81

nipple tassels, 73, 74, 75

nudity, 87

O

obsession, 12

ornamental, 21

P

Peekaboo, 57, 59, 63

personality, 2, 4

pleasure, 5, 13

protection, protective, 2, 3, 4

provocative, 4, 58

psychological, 2, 4, 5, 9, 12, 13, 38

purity, 14

R

radiate, 24, 52, 54, 70

rap, 41

refined, 4

retro-styled, 74

reveals, 86

risqué, 15

S

savored, 75

secret, 13, 77

security, 3

seduction, seductive, seductively, The Law of Seduction , 4, 5, 48, 52, 54, 55, 56, 57, 59, 65, 85

self-acceptance, 4

self-adornment, 12, 24, 40

self-concept, 2

self-conscious, 65

sensuality, sensual, sensually, 1, 10, 11, 15, 63, 69, 70

sex education, 30

sexuality, sexual, sexually, 1, 5, 9, 10, 15, 27, 29, 30, 34, 35, 37, 41, 47, 48, 49, 53, 55, 56, 59, 60, 63, 64, 70

Sexual Revolution, 5

sexy, sexier, 4, 72, 73, 82, 83

silhouette, 22, 23

sophisticated, 4

stimulating, stimulate, 11, 36, 53